DISCOVER YOUR HIDDEN BLESSING

UPJOHN AGHAJI

Discover Your Hidden Blessing

INSIGHT PUBLISHING

Copyright © 2017 Upjohn Aghaji
All rights reserved.
ISBN: 13: 978-0998927718
Insight Publishing, Georgia

DISCOVER YOUR HIDDEN BLESSING is published by Insight Publishing, LLC, 1600 Flat Shoals Rd. Se Atlanta, Georgia 30316

Scripture quotations are from the following versions: King James Version (KJV), the Amplified Bible (AMP), Berean Study Bible (BSB), Youngs Literal Translation (YLT) and the English Standard Version (ESV).

ALL RIGHTS RESERVED

Rights for publishing this book in other languages are contracted by Insight Publishing. No part of this publication may be reproduced, stored in a retrieval system, or transmitted, in any form. No copies shall be made electronically, mechanically, by photocopy or recording of any form without written permission.

Insight publishing is dedicated to providing well balanced teaching materials and gospel centered products for the edification of the church. Our scripturally balanced tools and easy to use materials will energize and empower believing churches to evangelize, disciple, minister to the youth and children while edifying the whole family. We prayerfully trust that our books will help you with true biblical discoveries and growth while helping others to grow.

DEDICATION

This book is dedicated to all that are seeking to have a closer walk with the Lord.

ACKNOWLEDGEMENTS

I am eternally indebted to Jesus Christ and forever thankful for the great blessing of the Holy Spirit.

Over the years, my wife Arlethea has stood by me as I worked through and learned more about this subject and for this I am grateful. Thanks to my daughter Chinelo, who helped to read through this work. Ashley and Upjohn Jr. were always around to encourage me.

I must also acknowledge Pastor Edward Cross Sr. and Gina Cross, who have been our pastors, good friends and mentors in the things of God over the years.

Finally, to the host of friends, brothers and sisters in Christ who were sounding boards as I continued the process of writing this book, thank you.

CONTENTS

	INTRODUCTION	1
Chapter One	THE BEATITUDES	7
Chapter Two	INSTANT BLESSING	22
Chapter Three	THE PROMISE	27
Chapter Four	WAITING FOR THE SEED	34
Chapter Five	BLESSING TIME!	40
Chapter Six	TIME TO GROW UP	45
Chapter Seven	WHERE LIES YOUR PRIORITY?	49
Chapter Eight	TRULY BLESSED	54
Chapter Nine	SPIRITUAL BLESSINGS	64
Chapter Ten	CHANGE OF LANGUAGE	73
Chapter Eleven	JABEZ AND A BLESSED LIFE	76
Chapter Twelve	BLESSING IN GIVING	84
Chapter Thirteen	CONCLUSION	89

"Christ hath redeemed us from the curse of the law, being made a curse for us: for it is written, cursed is everyone that hangeth on a tree: That the blessing of Abraham might come on the Gentiles through Jesus Christ; that we might receive the promise of the Spirit through faith"

(Galatians 3:13-14, KJV).

INTRODUCTION

The word "Bless" has possibly become one of the most misunderstood and abused words in the world. We even say, "Bless you" when someone sneezes, for reasons not readily identified. Seriously, though, most people in this world want to be blessed, feel already blessed or feel like they are going to be blessed. All categories of people have their own ideas of what it means to be "blessed". While this concept means different things to different people, it must be discerned properly. Because western culture is steeped in materialism, it is easy to use an object-oriented measurement for everything, even spiritual things. It never computes properly. Yet, this thought process has been successfully sown into most of modern society.

The natural harvest from such seed is that, when material increase is not your daily reality, questions arise. Some, at the extreme, question God's love or faithfulness altogether and at worst, disregard God's true blessing. Many well-meaning believers have been caught in this dangerous wave of gross error.

All the credit must be laid at the feet of the off

base, acquisitive teachings coming from earthly-minded, money hungry preachers whose god is their belly and their minds are set on earthly things (Philippians 3:18-19).

God is a God of blessing. No one can or should argue over that, but ... there is a "but". What does scripture tell us about this word bless or blessing? Does God always mean the same thing that the world means? The answer to this question will bring clarity and subsequently save many from living a life of stress and frustration. The way we answer this question will determine what kind of relationship we will have with God and with one another. We need to pause and ponder without distraction, or maybe we are too neck deep into our daily pursuits to contemplate such serious matters.

Today we have so many more means of seeing so many new things than ever before — magazines and television and malls, social media, and emails, for instance — and so many more mediums to choose from.

All of society seems to be set up to cater to and nurture the desire for more, more and much more. Since ads feature constantly on our TVs, computers, billboards, and are even delivered directly to our phones, there is always something more before us we should desire or need. So, we are left oftentimes feeling less satisfied and blessed than we should be. Candidly, the sense that material things amount to blessing has weakened the Church considerably and tampered with our singleness of focus and purpose. One says, "God blessed me with a house" while the other says "God blessed me with a car." While another says they are "waiting to be blessed." They will say things like "God will bless me with a job" or, "when God blesses me with my own home …" The core thought behind the "bless me" is usually "with" something material. Our atmosphere is so rife with this notion that it has become thoroughly disingenuous and an absolute threat to sound biblical values and impedes true spiritual pursuits. For this reason, the line has been blurred between the value system of the church and the world. The New Testament scriptures know no such talk. One cannot imagine Paul or Peter saying such things and most certainly not Jesus. Think about it. Have you read any words remotely similar in the New Testament? Something that would sound like, "God blessed me with a chariot" or "God blessed me with a farm?" The answer would have to be no. No one in that context ever said that they were blessed with a house, horse, farm or chariot, and there is a reason for that. And yes, you can always point to the Old Testament. However, please continue reading.

Before I go on, I must once and for all clearly state that I understand we need a home, cars and all that God has provided for us. Indeed, scripture lets us know that our Father has given us all these things to enjoy (1 Timothy 6:17). He also knows what we need. (Matthew 6:8). I stress this because, when teaching this legitimate approach to scripture, I am often told that we need *these* things. I am not sure why someone would think that this teaching suggests that things are not important. Of course they are, but I repeat, these are still things. Things are things. They are not comparable to God's blessing! This has to be known and appreciated.

Only the Holy Spirit filled child of God is blessed. If you are not one of those, you are lost and quite frankly, dead. No unbeliever is blessed, regardless of their financial status or their accomplishments, as far as the New Covenant is concerned. Anyone can acquire things but only believers are blessed, scripturally.

The word of God in our New Covenant speaks of "things" separately from blessing. You will explore the reasoning while reading these pages. This revelation will change your life. Keep in mind that according to Jesus, anyone, including unbelievers, can benefit from His benevolence and goodness materially and continue in their wicked and sinful condition. God does not discriminate when it pertains to possessions. He does allow his sun to shine on good and bad people. His rain falls on the just and unjust, according to Matthew 5:45.

"for He causes His sun to rise on the evil and the good, and sends rain on the righteous and the unrighteous."

However, if you don't know your God and maker, are you not bankrupt and in peril? Is that condition not worse than being cursed?

Surely, it is easy to see that anybody can partake in His material providence without being committed to Him, but you truly are blessed when you receive His indwelling presence. This is not to be taken lightly at all.

Please, patiently read the next few chapters with an open mind and let the scriptures enlighten us.

CHAPTER ONE

THE BEATITUDES

"When Jesus saw the crowds, He went up on the mountain; and when He was seated, His disciples came to Him. Then He opened His mouth and taught them saying. Blessed are the poor in spirit: for theirs is the kingdom of heaven" (Matthew 5:1-3, KJV).

In Matthew Chapter 5, Jesus saw the crowd following Him but He decided to go up the mountain. Prior to this in chapter 4, as He preached the gospel of the kingdom, He also showed compassion through healing and deliverance. He had just finished healing numerous people and His fame had travelled far. As a result, a substantial crowd had come from neighboring cities to be healed of different diseases and afflictions. Unlike many modern day preachers, the crowd did not even impress Him. His Father's time table was more important, so He withdrew Himself and climbed a mountain. Something else was on His mind and it was time to let it out. Could it be that He expected only the serious followers to go that far just to hear Him?

Maybe He sought to speak to more persistent seekers instead of the multitude who had come from neighboring cities as a result of His fame? It would take extra effort to go further just to hear His teaching on this occasion. This teaching was not for all but for only those willing to climb the literal mountain so they could be "elevated" spiritually. The teaching that would follow was for the ones who would go further in their search and yearning for truth.

The miracles were for all, but that moment was for the focused ones, willing to be inconvenienced by changing their position and exerting energy to climb to "higher ground." Likewise, this study is not for casual seekers or followers of Christ but for the ones who pursue spiritual growth. I have found that such people love the truth and are willing to reposition their minds when necessary. Such individuals are hungry, thirsty and ready to do what is required at any moment to make spiritual progress. This teaching is for you if you are willing to leave the ordinary and walk on a new level of faith and commitment with the Lord.

Why Jesus chose to deal with the subject of the blessed this early in His ministry we may not know for sure but must at least concede that it was very high on his priority list, considering He could have picked any other subject matter. So, "He taught them" the bible says; He provides an insight into His thoughts regarding the true state of blessedness, saying;

"Blessed are the poor in spirit"
(Matthew 5:2, KJV).

Keep in mind that the poor in spirit would not have been the blessed ones in the old economy, but going forward, these are the ones who will be happy. In other words, when he speaks of the blessed, the disciples should think in a new and more spiritual way. He saw this as necessary clarification to be made, considering that the scriptures did refer to material things also as blessings under the old covenant, which his hearers were familiar with. But now things are changing. A new standard is being laid down by our Lord. If you go down the rest of the chapter, you'll find that He continued to make more clarification on killing, for example, in Verses 21 and 22, saying,

*"Ye have heard that it was said of them **of old time**, Thou shalt not kill; and whosoever shall kill shall be in danger of the judgment: **But I say** unto you, That whosoever is angry with his brother without a cause shall be in danger of the judgment..."* (Matthew 5:21-22a, KJV).

He does the same with adultery in Verses 27 and 28. Such was the case with the word *bless* or *blessed*. The word here translated as *"blessed"* in the Greek is *makarios*, meaning happy or blessed. Therefore, Jesus is saying that if you want to be happy, you must have these qualities. These qualities will keep you happy regardless of what the world or life holds in store for you or throws at you.

We will read Matthew 5 from the Amplified (Classic Edition) bible for maximum clarity and unambiguity.

"Blessed (happy, to be envied, and spiritually

prosperous–with life-joy and satisfaction in God's favor and salvation, regardless of their outward conditions) are the poor in spirit (the humble, who rate themselves insignificant), for theirs is the kingdom of heaven!

Blessed and enviably happy [with a happiness produced by the experience of God's favor and especially conditioned by the revelation of His matchless grace] are those who mourn, for they shall be comforted [Isaiah 61:2]!

Blessed (happy, blithesome, joyous, spiritually prosperous–with life-joy and satisfaction in God's favor and salvation, regardless of their outward conditions) are the meek (the mild, patient, long-suffering), for they shall inherit the earth [Psalm 37:11]!

Blessed and fortunate and happy and spiritually prosperous (in that state in which the born-again child of God enjoys His favor and salvation) are those who hunger and thirst for righteousness (uprightness and right standing with God), for they shall be completely satisfied [Isaiah 55:1, 2]!

Blessed (happy, to be envied, and spiritually prosperous–with life-joy and satisfaction in God's favor and salvation, regardless of their outward conditions) are the merciful, for they shall obtain mercy!

Blessed (happy, enviably fortunate, and spiritually prosperous–possessing the happiness produced by the experience of God's favor and especially conditioned by the revelation of His grace, regardless of their outward conditions) are the pure in heart, for they shall see God [Psalm 24:3, 4]!

Blessed (enjoying enviable happiness, spiritually prosperous–with life-joy and satisfaction in God's Favor and salvation, regardless of their outward conditions) are the makers and maintainers of peace, for they shall be called the sons of God!

Blessed and happy and enviably fortunate and spiritually prosperous (in the state in which the born-again child of God enjoys and finds satisfaction in God's favor and salvation, (regardless of his outward conditions) are those who are persecuted for righteousness' sake (for being and doing right), for theirs is the kingdom of heaven!

Blessed (happy, to be envied, and spiritually prosperous–with life-joy and satisfaction in God's favor and salvation, regardless of your outward conditions) are you when people revile you and persecute you and say all kinds of evil things against you falsely on My account."

Be glad and supremely joyful, for your reward in heaven is great (strong and intense), for in this same way people persecuted the prophets who were before you" (Matthew 5:3-12 Amplified).

What a list. A totally different list from what they had been familiar with all along. This was radical teaching considering the old covenant mindset. This stunning list included the poor in spirit, the meek, the humble, the patient, the spiritually hungry, the merciful, mourners and peacemakers. This was a different list indeed.

Jesus makes it abundantly clear to His listeners that all who would be happy in this dispensation would be the spiritually rich. The Amplified version goes as far as adding in Verse 11, *"regardless of their outward conditions."*

Again,

"Blessed and happy and enviably fortunate and <u>spiritually prosperous</u> (in the state in which the born-again child of God enjoys and finds satisfaction in God's favor and salvation, <u>regardless of his outward conditions</u>).

The *"outward conditions"* were no longer as important? That is cardinal and central to the new thought He presented. He even taught that you were blessed when being persecuted or unjustly treated because of Him. How surprising was this to the Jewish audience to whom He spoke and I must add, to our modern preachers also. **Not one person on His list was blessed because of their possessions or worldly accomplishments**. All those were ephemeral and inconsequential as far as He was concerned.

It was the gumption of this thought that made His listeners think He was destroying the law. Further in the same chapter, in the seventeenth verse, we read the following words from Jesus,

*"****Do not think*** *that I have come to abolish the Law or the Prophets; I have not come to abolish them but to fulfill them"* (Matthew 5:17 ESV).

He obviously knew what they would be thinking. The teachers of the law especially would come out with guns blazing. It will be a hard pill to swallow because theological systems and economies have been built on the old teaching. That old and materialistic way of thinking, presupposes that material increase, respect with adulation awaits any *good* child of God. Jesus says, "*I have not come to abolish them but to fulfill them*". Yes, He came to fulfill the law. And we know that when something is fulfilled, we must go forward with the present reality. When a doctor writes a prescription, that paper is of tremendous value until the medication is filled. Jesus was getting to the heart of the matter, being that He was the solution to the human condition. He was not just a prescription but the fulfilment.

He knew their thoughts just as He knows yours right now. Jesus is relocating "blessing" to its proper place—on the inside. Sometimes our outward circumstances may not look too promising, yet you are blessed if your relationship with the Lord is unbroken. The Apostle Paul puts it beautifully here:

"**As sorrowful**, *yet always rejoicing*, **as poor**, *yet making many rich*, **as having nothing**, *and yet possessing all things*" (2 Corinthians 6:10).

When you have the Holy Spirit, you are blessed regardless of your human dilemma. Good or bad, you possess all things because your heavenly Father has made a commitment to spend eternity with you. Can you picture yourself with God and a host of other saints in a perfect world? A world with no robbers, no killers, no jealous folks and liars. He has promised you a new earth and a body that never deteriorates (1 Corinthians 15:41-44). This will erase sickness and death forever.

He dismisses stress and grief and abolishes fear and hatred. No more poverty when it is all over. This is the blissful forever existence that you have been guaranteed (John 10:10). You are in a good position and never will be at a loss regardless of your outward condition. All because Jesus paid the full price for your redemption and the Holy Spirit *in you,* is the guarantee, the earnest of God's wonderful promises. How could you be more blessed? You already have the best that God can offer, in the Holy Spirit. The Almighty has nothing better to offer you at this point. You have His absolute and eternal best — Himself, His Spirit.

All that is true assuming that you are saved. If not, you simply need Jesus to save and fill you with His Spirit. And as you grow in the Spirit, you will start to appreciate what you have been given. Many have not repented and reconnected with God. A huge percentage of the world are not filled with the Spirit of God and multitudes that have Him, never spend enough time with Him. No wonder they do not feel blessed. We really do need His touch now more than ever.

We experience Him through his touch, encouragement, direction, teaching, leading, comfort and healing. When you are healed of sickness and disease, it is just a reminder of the permanent healing coming when you receive your resurrection body, never to get sick again. That is where the Spirit of God is taking you. No more sickness and pain, no suffering and no more dying. The Spirit of God is committed to leading you to the other side of eternity where you can see more clearly without any blurred vision; whatever He reveals now is to keep you going until you can know as you are known (1 Corinthians 13:12). That is where He is taking you. He comforts us and encourages us never to give up through the many trials we experience in a twisted world. You ought to be always happy when your destiny is heaven. **Every believer has a bright future and all who will trust Him can be happy right now and in the world to come**. Your eternal destiny is His priority and that ought to be your priority also. This terrestrial existence is quite fleeting.

When God raised Jesus from the dead, it was His Spirit that He sent to do it (Romans 8:11). He makes it possible for you to overcome sin (Romans 8:13). You overcome sin by the power of the Holy Spirit given to you by Jesus. Sin is the barrier between you and your Maker. The Spirit of God empowers you to overcome any weakness. Whatever you struggle with today, the Spirit of Christ takes you beyond that and to God. This same Spirit resides in you because He has been mandated to bring you to God looking exactly like Jesus. He is "Christ in you." In fact, when you experience the Spirit of God, you are enlightened and you become one of those;

"… who have tasted the heavenly gift, and have shared in the Holy Spirit, and have tasted the goodness of the word of God and the powers of the age to come" (Hebrews 6:4, 5, English Standard Version).

He is the *heavenly gift*. He is also *the power of the world to come*. He gives you a taste of heaven right here, right now. He is the power of the age to come but you have Him right now with you. He has been mandated to bring you with Him back to the Father. He has come from the future to take you back to the future. He will and He can never fail because He is the Spirit of Christ. Christ never fails. He is the eternal power! He is the one walking with you, guiding you, upholding you, empowering you, strengthening you, comforting you, teaching you, reassuring you, praying through you and for you, helping you, and showing you things to come. Again, when you say the words "Christ in me," that's the Holy Spirit. He is the treasure in your earthen vessel. He is the advocate and the anointing. He literally is the Spirit of Christ and the Spirit of God at the same time.

While here in our sin-laden environment, He constantly reassures us that our real Father is the Almighty God. He must continue this important work, until you get back home with God your Father. So, we continue to cry Abba Father only by His Spirit (Romans 8:15).

"… you have received a spirit of adoption as sons by which we cry out, "Abba! Father!"

What a wonderful blessing He is. Through Jesus, by His Spirit we are adopted as God's children. We are "born again" into His family.

This is very significant because our minds are under constant attack by the enemy of our souls. He is always trying to discourage us and make us feel less than the blessed children of God that we are. All because of what happened in the garden with Adam and Eve. Yes, that's where it all started. God blessed His people and satan did not like it.

Remember Adam and Eve? God made and formed them, then breathed the "breath" of life into them, right? And later we read "and He blessed them." He breathed life-giving spirit into them when they were formed yet continued to "bless" them by speaking the refreshing word of blessing over them. This undoubtedly shows that it was always God's original intent for us to live a blessed life. But the enemy went to work on their minds. He sought to convince them that they needed more when they had it all.

A truly blessed person will be satisfied and live in real contentment. It is the adamic nature that pulls us into unhealthy materialistic lifestyles. Adam and Eve were not satisfied with God's instructions and provision. The same lack of contentment is the devil's premium tool in this modern age. It's this rapaciousness that breeds endless material pursuits. It remains the enemy's chief tool today. God has blessed us and we must stay grateful every day.

CHAPTER TWO

INSTANT BLESSING

"And God Blessed Them and Said Be Fruitful and Multiply" (Genesis 1:28).

Before the first family was created, everything they would need was made available to them. In Eden, the Lord put all that would be required for them to be happy and satisfied. God already knew and provided all of that, and more in abundance for them. To top it all off, He made Himself available to them always. He walked and talked with them. Yet in Verse 28, we read,

"and God blessed them."

God blessed them!

This ought to immediately show us that the

word "blessed" had nothing to do with the trees, the food nor the beautiful abode given to them eastward in Eden (Gen 2:8 KJV). Think about it, they had it all, a good marriage, food, no mortgage payments to make and good health. Everything on this earth was already provided for them. They had it all materially, yet it was still God's desire to *bless* them. He did not waste time in doing just that. No fanfare, just instant blessing. What was this blessing? Was it of a spiritual nature? Yes, it had to have been.

Now, note that the word rendered as "blessed" here according to Strong's dictionary is *barak*, meaning to bless, kneel, to be blessed, to bless oneself, to be adored, to congratulate or to salute.

It is easy to notice that this word barak, does not tell us much. It is a little vague because of the spiritual nature of this gesture. Spiritual things sometimes are hard to put in human words. The definition here seems to be more of manifestations of the blessing. For instance, causes one to *kneel*, to be *blessed* and so on. Several words in scripture defy human intellectual definitions in Greek, Hebrew, English or any language. Often, we simply rely on the expressions of spiritual endowments as a description. Merriam Webster thinks it is "to hallow or consecrate by religious rite or word." Such is also the case with words like curse, love, etc. For instance, 1 Corinthians 13, tells us that,

"love is patient and kind; love does not envy or boast; it is not arrogant or rude; it does not insist on its own way" 1 Corinthians 13:4 (ESV Bible).

Yes, a loving person is patient but some mean individuals patiently stalk their victims also. However, the love of God is a spiritual endowment that one cannot claim to have while being pushy and short fused with loved ones and so on. Love, just like bless is a spiritual endowment flowing from the empowerment of His Spirit. So, what we know for sure is that "bless" in this verse or context did not necessarily refer to material things and only gives impetus to the rest of the statement in Verse 28. "… *be fruitful and multiply*, etc."

The original family was to fill their new abode with more blessed inhabitants, cultivate it and partake in the enjoyment. That was all that the Lord asked of them. Stay away from the tree.

Simply maintain what He gave them and keep on enjoying life. Their fruitfulness would come from the multiplication of God's already created substance. This pronunciation of beatitude simply gave an assurance of God's favor and approval to carry His grace. They simply were to carry on with the creative work based on what the ultimate creator had put in place. What a noble task they had.

Anyway, Adam and Eve were lured into dissatisfaction, like many of us, and were tempted to disobey. They took the blessing for granted and they fell in Genesis Chapter 3. God curses the serpent but not Adam or Eve. He cursed the ground but not His people. What a loving Father. But, although man was not cursed by the creator, things around him were cursed and untold hardship was ahead. The punitive consequences of sin would be severe. Childbirth would be painful and obtaining sustenance would be hard and achieved with much sweat. Things changed after the fall. The consequences of sin were far reaching. You see, when sin is present, it challenges our ability to feel blessed. All creation also suffers as a result. God did not change, but sin changed everything. It altered how they saw God and themselves. Then it changed how they related to the world around them, and the things that God had made for them. We all inherited this weakness from our ancestors Adam and Eve.

This is how sin entered the world and death followed ultimately. Our priorities became inherently mixed up. Instead of humanity enjoying a perpetual state of blessedness, we struggle to live and experience unnecessary turmoil and stress. Many turn to all the wrong things instead of building a relationship with their loving creator and one another. The thinking is that they can be comfortable here as they amass more stuff. How sensible is that in a sinful world filled with selfishness, envy, greed and much pollution? What is your priority in this life? Where does your focus lie?

Nonetheless, our Father's plan has not changed. We only need to recognize his plan. God loves us immensely and is determined to see all of us blessed if only we would listen to His word. Don't allow the world to tell you different.

CHAPTER THREE

THE PROMISE

After the fall, Adam failed to convey this blessing to the rest of humanity. God later made a firm promise of blessing to Abraham in Genesis 22 in response to Abraham's obedience to the voice of God. This time, it will not be like the garden. The seed would be the second Adam, Jesus (1 Corinthians 15:45). He will be accomplishing this for all humanity.

Through this seed of Abraham, real blessing will come again into the world. Now, this blessing is guaranteed to be more efficacious and permanent. God will ensure that the blessing will be available to everyone who will be willing to receive. Our Father is not depending on frail humans anymore but on His own Son—the seed. So, we read,

"And in thy seed shall all the nations of the earth be

blessed; because thou hast obeyed my voice" (Genesis 22:18, KJV).

The seed would convey the blessing to the nations. In other words, the vehicle through which the blessing comes to us. The seed was Jesus, the Holy Spirit would be in Jesus without measure and once Jesus went back to the Father, this holy blessing would touch the whole world! Jesus contained the blessing. You will see this more clearly as you read further.

Because of Adam and his wife's episode with the fruit in the garden, our loving Father set in motion a more sure way to bring us to that state of blessedness forever! He never changed his mind about blessing humanity but this would now be accomplished in and through the seed of Abraham. So, we read in Genesis 22:18, KJV,

"And in thy seed shall all the nations of the earth be blessed."

God reveals the assurance of this coming blessing to Abraham. He announces how the great blessing will be accomplished after the fall. Everyone wants to be blessed. And this time, it will be brought to us by Jesus the Son, so we can live in a perpetually blessed state. This means that, until the manifestation of the expected seed of Abraham, Jesus, there could not possibly be any true blessing. Only a promise and pursuit of shadows was possible.

Jacob wanted to be blessed just like us. His strong desire led him to struggle for a whole night with a divine being. Without being able to articulate what he actually was asking for, Jacob would not let go until he is blessed. Like many of us, the sensed presence of deity presents a chance to ask for something — anything or whatever we want. Knowing him, he probably wanted protection from his brother or enemies and wanted more stuff like many today. But, he only needed to be reminded that God had been protecting and keeping him all along his journey.

Notwithstanding, with a dislocated joint, he continues to struggle with the being. He will not let go until he is blessed, still not articulating what he meant by "bless me". He obtains a new name instead, and his life is forever changed. It might not have been what he expected, but it was in God's plan and it was what he needed. As a direct result of this event, he was no longer known as a grabber or supplanter, rather he becomes the birth of the nation—Israel, meaning, "God prevails." Is God calling you to some higher purpose? Are you, like Jacob, praying for material things as blessings? Let the Almighty prevail with His purpose for your life. Amen. Or are you like Esau who was too focused on natural hunger while despising his spiritual heritage—his blessing. Esau was robbed of his spiritual right, so we are warned not to be like him. Let us hunger for the real satisfaction, the true bread and the real blessing—the Spirit. Only He, Jesus the seed, can accomplish this in our lives.

Over time, many prophets looked for the promise. Malachi prophesied about the promised blessing and the prophets kept on looking ahead for it. They may not have fully known what it was all about, but they perceived that something big was going to happen upon this earth. God was going to save and bless His people. God Himself, through the prophet Malachi, went as far as saying,

*"… prove me now herewith, saith the LORD of hosts, if I will not open you the windows of heaven, and pour you out **a blessing**, that there shall not be room enough to receive it"* (Malachi 3:10b, KJV).

Please note that "blessing" here is in the singular. Not blessings but "*a blessing,*" as in one specific blessing very likely pointing to the Spirit. Furthermore, the said blessing is "*poured*" out from heaven, making it of a tangible spiritual essence. I cannot imagine God speaking of pouring out material things from heaven, can you? It will be poured out like rain. Rain represents the Spirit in scripture, (Hosea 6:3). The home, the city and indeed the world does not have enough room for the blessing of His Spirit.

In considering this text, we should keep in mind that Malachi was a prophet who spoke of present and future events. The physical rain foreshadowed the pouring of God's Spirit on man. But the Father would require present obedience from Malachi's contemporaries. The creator would "pour out" a blessing that would change the Jewish nation including the whole known and unknown world. This was no limited blessing that can be contained and managed in your small dwelling. You alone cannot contain this, they cannot contain this, no one individual, no one church, denomination or city, country or continent alone can contain the heavenly promise because Malachi spoke also of the "pouring out" of the Holy Spirit! Are you starting to embrace the truth yet? You see, God constantly spoke through the prophets regarding the coming glories He had in store for us. The prophets wondered who the individuals were that would live this experience. That's why Peter reminds us that the prophets kept on, as scripture states;

"inquiring what person or time the Spirit of Christ in them was indicating when he predicted the **sufferings of Christ and the subsequent glories**" (1 Peter 1:11, ESV).

Peter continues to say that;

"It was revealed to them that they were serving not themselves but **you**, *in the things that have now been announced to you through those who preached the good news to* **you** *by the* **Holy Spirit sent from heaven**, *things into which angels long to look"* (1 Peter 1:12, ESV).

Even the angels longed to look into these things that pertain to us. How wonderful is this? You are in a unique spiritual position regarding your salvation. You are uniquely, thoroughly and supremely blessed. Paul puts it in this manner in Romans chapter 4;

"**Blessed** are those whose lawless deeds are forgiven, and whose sins are covered; **blessed** is the man against whom the Lord will not count his sin." Romans, 4: 7-8 (ESV).

Remarkably, our heavenly Father had to clean the vessel to fill us with his presence. There ought to be no doubt in your mind that the Holy Spirit is the best possible gift any individual can receive. No one can say that Jesus is Lord except by His Spirit. (1 Corinthians 12:3).

CHAPTER FOUR

WAITING FOR THE SEED

While waiting for the appointed time for the seed to be revealed, the law was put in place under the Old Covenant. This covenant with the Israelites was essentially materialistic and was meant to serve them until the revelation of the seed. They clearly were told in no uncertain terms that blessing was related to land inheritance;

*"For **those blessed by Him will inherit the land,** But **those cursed by Him will be cut off.**"* (Psalm 37:22) KJV.

Under this law period, curses came with serious disobedience. The curse was to be *"cut Off"*. Whenever the words of the law were read, it came with blessing and cursing. The fear of being cursed competed with blessings.

*"Then afterward he read all the words of the law, **the blessing and the curse**, according to all that is written in the book of the law."* Joshua 8:34.

The law came with curses and humanity would need to look to God for a solution. There was always the constant reminder that they were a step away from disaster even when they were experiencing material progress from God. Again, we read in Deuteronomy 11:29;

*"It shall come about, when the LORD your God brings you into the land where you are entering to possess it, **that you shall place <u>the blessing</u> on Mount Gerizim and <u>the curse</u> on Mount Ebal**."*

This explains why much of what we read under the Old Covenant was pointing toward the future. The New Covenant was called "a better covenant," the superior covenant based on better promises.

"But as it is, Christ has obtained a ministry that is as much more excellent than the old as the covenant he mediates is better, since it is enacted on better promises." (Hebrews 8:6)

Also, we see that the law made nothing perfect while the old annulled commandment was weak and did not offer much hope. We read;

"For there is verily an annulling of the former commandment because of the weakness and unprofitableness thereof. For the law made nothing perfect, but the bringing in of a better hope did, by which we draw nigh unto God." Hebrews 7:18, 19.

To read further on the New Covenant, look for my earlier book "The Hidden Covenant Revealed"

The point here is that the seed was needed to bring man into the full promise of God. The promises had genuine and spiritually discernable eternal weight attached to it. Blessing without any curse attached to it. So then, while waiting for the seed, everything under the law was a foreshadow;

"The Law is only a shadow of the good things to come, not the realities themselves." (Hebrews 10:1) Berean Study Bible.

Circumcision under the law was a foreshadow of better things: The temple was a foreshadow; the priesthood was a foreshadow; likewise, the material blessings were all foreshadows of the real blessing to come. The manna was a foreshadow of Jesus; therefore, could not satisfy the hungry but for a moment. In the same manner, all the material blessings of old put together could not satisfy the recipient. The law itself could not make anyone measure up to God's expectation (Hebrews 10:1b) but the seed will change everything.

Marrying many women, annexing other nations' land, winning all kinds of military campaigns would never satisfy the human soul. No amount of material bounty would satisfy. All these had curses lurking around and the fear of judgment. Only this one great and eternal blessing, the Spirit of God through the seed, Jesus, would have eternal value and eternally sustaining power. This is the blessing with no curse attached. God has revealed this great blessing to us in his word clearly.

The word of God clearly reveals that the law was given only until the seed would come. It was as transgressions grew and were getting out of hand, that the law was introduced. We read in the book of Galatians,

"Wherefore then serveth the law? It was added because of transgressions, **till the seed should**

come to whom the promise was made..." (Galatians 3:19, KJV).

The law came 430 years after God made the promise of blessing that would come through Abraham's seed. It did not tamper with the promise but simply was there to lead us to Christ. Because it is only in Him that we would be truly blessed.

Listen to Paul the apostle inspired by God as he explains that;

"This is what I mean: the law, which came 430 years afterward, does not annul a covenant previously ratified by God, so as to make the promise void" (Galatians 3:17, KJV).

The law was a custodian that brought us to Him — Jesus. Again, we read,

"But before faith came, we were kept under the law, shut up unto the faith which should afterwards be revealed. Wherefore **the law was our schoolmaster to bring us unto Christ**, *that we might be justified by faith."* (Galatians 3:23, 24).

As stated earlier, the law dispensed blessings and curses depending on behavior. In Deuteronomy 28, the two sides are clearly outlined. The Spirit of God does not curse us at all instead He picks us up and encourages us when we fall. Living under the law was equal to being under a curse as scripture states;

*"For **as many as are of the works of the law are under the curse**; for it is written, **'Cursed is everyone who does not continue in all things which are written in the book of the law**, to do them'"* (Galatians 3:10).

Because no one could keep all the law. There had to be another way to be blessed. Think about it. It all meant that, no matter how blessed they felt, the curse was always waiting somewhere close by. But something better was coming. The great blessing would be revealed through Jesus Christ, because the word said, "in the seed," which is our Lord. The comforter was coming!

This is literally the blessing of the New Covenant in Christ… the Holy Spirit with all the spiritual bounties He comes with. The Spirit was in the seed. The seed would be Jesus.

CHAPTER FIVE

BLESSING TIME!

"But when the fullness of the time was come, God sent forth his Son, made of a woman, under the law" (Galatians 4:4).

The good news today is that you can be blessed right now. The fulness of time did eventually come and God did what He said He would do. Scripture says that, *"God sent forth his Son"*.

Many of us are already blessed but do not know it. For this reason, some still live in fear, anxiety, depression, confusion, sinfulness, unhappiness, frustration, oppression and regression because we pay undue and undeserved attention to our circumstances. You must get hold of this truth! This is wonderful, the real blessing is here reaching out to you. His grace has been sent down through His son Jesus to you. That is the gospel. We are reminded of this truth when Paul wrote to the Galatian church stating;

*"And the scripture, foreseeing that God would justify the heathen through faith, preached before **the gospel** unto Abraham saying, **In thee shall all nations be blessed**"* (Galatians 3:8, KJV).

The gospel of Jesus is also the gospel of blessing. The same gospel was preached to Abraham long before now. How I pray that the gospel will once again be focused on Christ and what he, and only he, has done for us. How I pray that humanity will discover the real blessing *in* Christ. It is like a *hidden blessing* that is distant from the unspiritual but nearer to the spiritually hungry and the spiritually needy. As we crave real satisfaction in our lives, we think it is a house, and find we are not satisfied. We think it is the car, but we are left looking for something else. When we think we have it all, something else goes wrong somewhere. When all is well, we still die. This proves frustrating until we are freed by this revelation. The good news is that this is your time to be eternally blessed. God has sent His son. True happiness is now possible in Christ. Let me put it in another way; We can embrace happiness, joy and peace in the Holy Ghost regardless of outward circumstances. Every believer must truly believe and say;

"to live is Christ and to die is gain" (Philippians 1:21, KJV).

For the Spirit filled believer, all is gain and life is Christ. With the Holy Spirit, we can rejoice in good and bad times. We count our trials as joyful. Why would the scriptures say, "count it all joy when you fall into various trials" if it is not possible? No one can do this without the Spirit of God in them. Nothing in this realm can match the divine blessing in store for all who would seek Him. All the glories and failures of this life will always mean nothing in His presence.

Go ahead and invite Him into your life now and forever be blessed. Ask Jesus to come into your life and let Him fill you with His Spirit right now. That's exactly what He will do. He will bless you with His presence. The whole world needs the blessing. Jesus has cleared the way for us to return to our Father to receive from Him this wonderful fulfillment of His promise. We are now His and should live in absolute fulfilment and joy. The promises of our God are guaranteed. So, if you ask, you shall receive and if you seek, you shall find. There is no more need to go through life frustrated. It does not matter what your circumstances are, you can live a blessed life now and forever.

I write these words out of experience. I have been through things in my lifetime; mistakes, disappointments from friends and family, betrayal of trust and more. So many of us have been through illness, pain and loss, but the Holy Spirit has made a world of difference. He is the ultimate partner and confidant. I cannot say enough about His love and warmth. He is always pointing me toward Jesus and revealing the Father daily in his word. No one can comfort you like Him, no one can encourage you like Him. He will make you laugh at trials and dance in the midst of trouble. Jesus Himself explained to His disciples that it was important that He left this earth so that they would have the Holy Spirit,

*"Nevertheless, I tell you the truth: **it is to your advantage that I go away**, for if I do not go away,*

the Helper will not come to you. But if I go, I will send him to you" (John 16:7, ESV).

The Holy Spirit is the Spirit of God and at the same time, the Spirit of Christ as stated earlier. He captures the essence of God and wants to dwell in you and express the life of God through us. I assure you that He will love you and touch others through you. As you make yourself available, you will appreciate the spirit of Jesus' words. You will know for sure that you are a child of God. Scripture says that,

"… if anyone does not have the Spirit of Christ, he does not belong to Him" (Romans 8:9).

This is no small matter. It is not an abstract concept. You totally need Him.

CHAPTER SIX

TIME TO GROW UP

It is time to grow up! God is speaking to us right now requiring us to mature spiritually. Our appreciation for spiritual things should be more than our affection for the material.

"If then you have been raised with Christ, seek the things that are above, where Christ is, seated at the right hand of God. **Set your minds on things that are above, not on things that are on earth.** *For you have died, and your life is hidden with Christ in God. When Christ who is your life appears, then you also will appear with him in glory."* (Colossians 3:1-4)

Time is running out and the Church needs to focus. For too long in recent history, the church has functioned on a lower maturity level. Hopefully we will understand that we **are** living in the end times and every worldly distraction must be checked. It's time to grow up. We need spiritual meat and not candies thrown out to pacify spiritual children. We are living in a different dispensation. In the New Covenant dispensation, God is speaking to us differently.

He spoke to His people under the Old Covenant as less mature. The reason is that humanity was in a spiritually infantile stage. The old covenant was characteristically a materialistic one. The law was written in actual stone rather than the heart of man. In the old economy, good behavior was rewarded with materially tangible rewards. It is quite similar to the way you would relate to your growing child. You would promise them candy if they behaved; but in fact, you are training them to mature and become prepared and productive. The Lord would in such manner, promise them land, good produce and so on for good behavior. Bad behavior was punished and the cycle would continue.

Some of the bad behavior of your child is often looked upon as immaturity and ignorance or "growing pains." Scripture says that God at such times and in certain situations, ignored man's folly and spiritual short sightedness.

*"And the times of this ignorance **God winked** at; **but now** commandeth all men everywhere to repent"* (Acts 17:30, KJV).

Man would make graven images and carved idols to worship as their God. They were devoting their worship to things they could see and touch. The mystery of Christ, yet to be revealed, was kept secret for generations. They felt that God favored them only at times of material prosperity. People saw material success as the manifestation of God's favor and blessing. What childishness.

Really, nothing could be further from the truth; but, the same is sadly the case today. We must repent and mature now. Our Lord is calling us to a higher place. We can now partake in the promised blessing in and through Christ. Our loving Father is now communicating with us as grownups. He *"commandeth all men everywhere to repent."* Change your mind, change the direction of your thoughts and direct them towards God because you can. This is the spiritual reality that the Lord is bringing to us right now. The time for change is now and this message is for you. Let all of us together, put away all childish thinking and pursue the Lord with all our heart. Spiritual maturity is not suggested but required from us. For too long, the world has looked at the children of God with amusement as we go about pursuing the same things they crave. What is the difference between the believer and unbeliever if we keep saying that material things are blessings? Why will the unsaved rich man want to be blessed? He will think and say that he already is more blessed than a believer, while pointing at his big home and luxury cars.

Our language matters and the Christian should stop speaking like perpetual children. Candy is not real food. It is only sweet in the mouth and not in the belly. Real nutritious food may not have much sugar but will help you grow. Candy is for kids meat is for adults. Grow up. I will put it in the apostle's words;

"When I was a child, I spoke as a child, I understood as a child, I thought as a child; but when I became a man, I put away childish things." (1Corinthians 13:11) KJV.

How we speak of material things and blessing does matter. The secular world is listening.

CHAPTER SEVEN

WHERE LIES YOUR PRIORITY?

The patriarchs expected blessing to come from preceding generations. Blessing was not just something they found in personal success, instead they thought that personal success depended on this invocation. It customarily was not something that was given in tangibles but usually spoken on an individual. It required them to be in the parents' or predecessor's good graces. It was about relationship. Bad behavior brought a curse as in the case of Noah and sons or God and the Jews.

Notice the following; Jacob tricked his father to get it. Jacob struggled all night to receive his blessing. Esau was ready to kill Jacob for it being that it was not replaceable. Esau could not replace it after the loss. It could only come from his father, not his job, his business or himself. In the same manner, Esau's father could not retrieve it from Jacob to confer it back on Esau.

True blessing can only come from our Father-God. We must be reconciled to Him to be blessed. Are you hungry to be filled now? Do you yearn for Him? You want the Holy Spirit because that is the one relationship that you can never lose. You may lose your friends, family and home, lose your car, but the Spirit of God will never leave you. He will walk with you and help you at all times and forever.

Also, the patriarchs knew that the blessing was what gave them legitimacy regarding an inheritance. Likewise, in God's kingdom, the blessing, who is the Holy Spirit, gives you legitimacy. Remember, the blessing that Jacob's father placed on him, for all intents and purposes, made Jacob the legitimate heir; although, Esau was supposed to be the one. It was for this very reason that Esau was murderously angry with his brother, because that kind of blessing was, as mentioned earlier, irreversible. God has given His Spirit as a down payment for His "purchased possessions", which will be His people. You and I.

Ephesians 1:13 and 14 says; *"In whom ye also trusted, after that ye heard the word of truth, the gospel of your salvation: in whom also after that ye believed, ye <u>were sealed with that holy Spirit of promise</u>, which is **the earnest of our inheritance** until the redemption of the purchased possession, unto the praise of his glory."*

Our Father has bestowed on us an irreversible blessing that makes us the legal heirs of everything that God has for us in his kingdom. It confirms our birthright! So, we read again,

"... *if children, Heirs also*, **heirs of God and fellow heirs with Christ**, *if indeed we suffer with Him so that we may also be glorified with Him"* (Romans 8:17, New American Standard Bible).

We are His because we are blessed with His Spirit. What a blessed assurance. The scope here overshadows all the other "blessings" seen in the Old Testament. So, how important is the blessing? We will simply say that nothing else is more important.

Our heavenly Father knew what he was doing when he gave the Holy Spirit without measure to Jesus. He was to fill all of us with His Spirit. The time to *pour the Spirit* had finally come and Jesus would lead the way.

*"For he whom God has sent utters the words of God, **for he gives the Spirit without measure**. The Father loves the Son and has given all things into his hand. Whoever believes in the Son has eternal life; whoever does not obey the Son shall not see life, but the wrath of God remains on him"* (John 3:34-36, ESV).

You can have the Holy Spirit today by giving your life to Jesus Christ. We are now living in the richest dispensation that man has ever known. You do not have to be frustrated and defeated by life. You can be blessed. Jesus has the Spirit without measure and he is waiting to pour out to all that thirst and yearn for God's blessing. He is not sprinkling but pouring and filling all that would ask.

You may have the irreversible and eternal blessing from God. Our blessing is superior to the patriarchs'. Go ahead and ask, as Jesus said to his disciples;

"For every one that asketh receiveth, and he that seeketh findeth, and to him that knocketh it shall be

*opened. If a son shall ask bread of any of you that is a father, will he give him a stone? Or if he ask a fish, will he for a fish give him a serpent? Or if he shall ask for an egg, will he offer him a scorpion? If ye then, being evil, know how to give good gifts unto your children, how much more shall your heavenly Father **give the holy Spirit** to them that ask Him"* (Luke 11:10-13, KJV).

Everyone is able and qualified to receive. All you need is to ask Him into your life. So many have received Jesus and are living the blessed life already, what about you? Again, He says,

"And it shall come to pass in the last days, saith God, I will pour out of my Spirit upon all flesh" (Acts 2:17, KJV).

This is the pouring time — not the squirting time, but a real shower time in the Spirit. "All flesh" includes you and your household and friends. Everyone.

CHAPTER EIGHT

TRULY BLESSED

"Christ hath redeemed us from the curse of the law, being made a curse for us: for it is written, Cursed is everyone that hangeth on a tree: That **the blessing of Abraham** *might come on the Gentiles through Jesus Christ; that we might* **receive the promise of the Spirit** *through faith"* (Galatians 3:13-14, KJV).

Now, let us look closely at the above scripture. The apostle Paul is dealing with those who, having embraced the faith of Jesus Christ, still thought to continue seeking justification by the works of the law. This was folly he insisted. It would mean going backwards to kindergarten. No, it was worse than that, it was an attempt to go back to curses. No one who has the Spirit of God through faith in Christ Jesus will want to go backwards unless they were "bewitched" and deceived. No person in their right minds wants to deal with curses unless they were under a spell.

In these verses, we are told in no uncertain terms that the Holy Spirit is the blessing! We see these beautiful words in Galatians 3:13-14.

"Christ hath redeemed us from the curse of the law, being made a curse for us"

So, here are the plain facts:

What did Christ do?

He *"has redeemed us from the curse of the law."* (Galatians 3:13).

No more curses from the law. That's it. We are truly blessed! The law came with curses that we would have had to contend with. But now, no matter what our failures and challenges are, in Christ we are not and never will be cursed. No one, no pastor, no enemy, no witch or wizard can curse us. God will not and the devil cannot. Go ahead and rejoice. The fact of the matter is that Jesus did not *just* redeem us from sin, but He redeemed us also from the *curse of the law*. Going back to the law would mean also going back to the curses that follow disobedience. It was under the law that material things could be deemed blessings because everything in the Old Covenant was temporal. There was no real blessing because the Spirit of God was not yet filling everyone who asked. Jesus had not paid for the curse to be removed and Messiah was still on His way to save and bless humanity. His blood was yet to be shed.

He hung on a tree for one reason:

*"that the **blessing** of Abraham might come on the Gentiles."* (Galatians 3:14a)

Did you hear that? The blessing of Abraham not blessings. The long-awaited blessing promised to all nations is here now. This was promised to Abraham and is now being fulfilled in us and for us. Glory to God! Jesus has paid the price for us to be saved, rescued from curses and blessed. God always keeps His word and this time is no different.

What is that blessing?

"The promise of the Spirit." (Galatians 3:14b)

This is clearly spelled out right here. The Holy Spirit is the promise we have in Christ. He is **the** blessing of the New Covenant. Again, we read,

"that we might receive the promise of the Spirit..."

How do we receive?

"Through faith."

Through faith in Jesus! In Him alone can you be blessed.

Young's Literal Translation bible puts it this way,

*"that to the nations the blessing of Abraham may come in Christ Jesus, <u>**that the promise of the Spirit we may receive**</u> through the faith"* (Galatians 3:13-14, YLT).

Did you hear that? The Holy Spirit is not just a blessing but **the blessing**. What are you waiting for? Are you not convinced that you are blessed? If you have His Spirit, go ahead and thank the Lord. But if you do not have His Spirit, then ask the Lord to give you the blessing right now so you can be filled. The true "blessing of Abraham" is not in land or children or wealth. God gave him and his natural descendants land and wealth. But, contrary to the popular teachings, Abraham's real blessing is the Spirit of God. That's what all the nations of the world, Jews and Gentiles alike have received through his obedience. The real blessing of promise is in Jesus Christ. The Spirit of the Father is our blessing. The Spirit of Jesus. The blood of Jesus saves and qualifies us for blessing. Some may ask;

Are We Not Blessed When We Put God First?

Someone may say, what about Matthew 6:33? Over many years of teaching, I have been asked the same question in different forms such as; "Does the word not promise blessings for putting God first in our lives?" Well, let's look at the verse associated with this thought:

"But seek ye first the kingdom of God, and his righteousness; and all these **things** *shall be added unto you"* (Matthew 6:33).

The words, "all these **things**" do not in any way mean "all these blessings." The "things" mentioned here refer to the very things that the ungodly occupy their time and lives with.

Actually, it is the same preoccupation that this writing seeks to deliver us from. Things are neutral. They can be good or bad depending on who has possession. A house is a thing that can be a home, a fellowship hall or a whore-house. A knife can be used to cook or murder, depending on who has it. Money could be good or bad depending on what you do with it. But even more so, things can drown you just like water. Water is good and necessary; however, too much will intoxicate and even drown you.

God does provide things for us when we seek Him first, but He also helps those who do not seek Him first. He extends His goodness to them while expecting that they will be drawn to Him eventually. After all, they breathe His oxygen although he can stop that at any time but He doesn't. So, there is a real difference here. Our Father is good to all but only His children are blessed.

You can only be blessed spiritually according to New Testament scripture. The point of Matthew 6 is for us not to be fixated on material things like the unsaved person;

"These things dominate the thoughts of unbelievers,

***but your heavenly Father already knows** all your needs."* Matthew 6:32 NLT.

It is no longer a secret that God wants us to meditate on Him and dominate our thoughts with thoughts of Him. Therefore, the person who is filled with the Holy Spirit cannot be any more blessed even while momentarily passing through hard times in this life. Even when we are dealing with stressful relationships, financial, family or health issues. When compared to our heavenly hope and our heavenly gift, all your troubles are light afflictions and your whole lifetime is a moment. With eternity in view, you can persevere and endure anything.

"For our light affliction, which is but for a moment, worketh for us a far more exceeding and eternal weight of glory" (2 Corinthians 4:17, KJV).

So, keep on fighting the good fight, keep on pressing, keep on standing on his word. Keep on trusting. God has not forgotten you. He is forever faithful. Rejoice and be exceedingly glad, God is in you and with you and we are on our way to eternal bliss. We can live now by faith. Though some situations will change miraculously by God's precious power and some may not, but He will always give us enough grace to bear it. In all, we win! We know He can heal, fix and restore but, no matter what we face, we are blessed. We have the comforter with us. We can see through dark times with eyes of faith. His grace is sufficient. Pursue Him, seek Him now and immerse yourself in Him and allow Him to fill you.

When we have this attitude, He manifests Himself through us in healing, revelation and wisdom. Seek Him and not just what He can do. Everything must pale around Him. Let Him touch others as He overflows through your life. Start inviting others to be blessed. Become a conduit for this most treasured blessing. If we can receive this teaching, the energy with which we engage in some meaningless pursuits will be directed to the pursuit of God. We will spend more time being happy and counting it all joy instead of being depressed. So, get up, keep on moving, keep on working and keep on trusting our Lord. Amen! We will experience the blessed life here and later for eternity. We will experience God right this moment in a new most intimate way in our lives. Stand firm in Him. Refuse to be moved and controlled by circumstances and things. Start using your time on earth wisely.

Are There Some Blessed Unbelievers?

No. Not at all. You see, when properly discerned, the unbeliever will see that they will never be blessed apart from Christ. There is no blessed unbeliever. Remember this scripture?

"Whoever believes in the Son has eternal life; whoever does not obey the Son shall not see life, but the wrath of God remains on him" (John 3:36, ESV).

One's affluence, good health, wonderful family and great job all end here. True happiness comes from within, when your eternity is secure. The blessing of God is the key to real and everlasting joy. There is no blessed unbeliever because they do not have His Spirit. I do not envy any unsaved person regardless of their possessions or position in this life.

No More Stress?

Yes! Absolutely, the believer should no longer be stressed regarding whatever the world may throw at us. We can be more appreciative of what the Lord has done for us; therefore, we love and praise Him more. Our fellowship with the Spirit of God must become priority; hence, living a more fulfilled and spiritually vibrant life. Rejoice and again I say rejoice. Be filled with His Holy Spirit. Be encouraged and keep moving and living in God's plan and purpose for your life. You are blessed as long as He is with you.

CHAPTER NINE

SPIRITUAL BLESSINGS

*"Blessed be the God and Father of our Lord Jesus Christ, who **hath blessed us** with **all spiritual blessings** in heavenly places In Christ"*
(Ephesians 1:3, KJV).

God has blessed us! He is not waiting to bless us later. We do not need to ask Him to bless us. If Jesus is your Lord and God is your Father, you are already blessed. Fully and infinitely blessed. No further requirements other than being His child because you have His Spirit. You cannot be cursed. This word "blessings" here, refers to the believer's consecration to God. Blessings in Ephesians 1:3 is a translation of the Greek word eulogy, and it means "to speak well of." Considering that God is the one performing this eulogy, we can assert that God has and continues to speak good things regarding us and upon us. In other words, He has pronounced good things for our welfare, benefit and betterment. (Ephesians 1:4-13). All, of a spiritual nature in this context. There is a reason why God specifically said "**spiritual**" blessings. The word of God could have quite easily read "material" blessings. But it doesn't and never does throughout the whole New Testament.

You cannot possess "all spiritual blessings" without the Holy Spirit within. These are in the form of spiritual possessions, experiences and realities that only the Spirit will bring you into. It is the Spirit of God who communicates, exposes and applies these profound truths with heavenly ramifications to us through our spirit and ultimately to our life. These spiritual blessings are only available to the blessed ones who already have his Spirit. Hallelujah! Here is where I ask you to be a little patient while we take a more studious look at this verse.

Listen to some of the leading scholars of the New Testament. In Ellicott's commentary for English readers, Charles Ellicott holds a similar view on the same scripture, Ephesians

1:3. He also sees the spiritual nature of blessing when he wrote thus;

"God blesses us in real and life-giving "spiritual blessing," **i.e., blessing of the gift of the Spirit, for which we can return nothing except thanksgiving."**

-Charles John Ellicott

Mr. Ellicott believes that the life-giving blessing, *is of the Spirit*. I would like to add that these are also life changing blessings.

Another scholar that I thought had something important to say in this matter is Mr. MacLaren. In MacLaren's Commentary, we read once more;

"I do want to lay stress upon this, that, when the Apostle speaks about 'spiritual blessings,' he does not merely use that word 'spiritual' as defining the region in us in which the blessings are given, though that is also implied; but rather as pointing to the medium by which they are conferred. That is to say, he calls them 'spiritual,' not because they are, unlike material and outward blessings, gifts for the inner man, the true self, but because **they are imparted to the waiting spirit by that Divine**

Spirit *who communicates to men all the most precious things of God.* **They are 'spiritual' because the Holy Spirit is the medium of communication by which they reach men's spirits."**

MacLaren continues to say;

"For it is the Father who is the Giver, the Son who is the Reservoir, the Spirit who is the Communicator, of these spiritual gifts"

(1) all that the Father can bestow;

(2) all that the Son can provide;

(3) all that the Spirit can apply.

The resources of all the three Persons thus conspire to bless the Church."
-Alexander MacLaren

Mr. Joseph Benson does more in his Commentary. He is more in depth on this verse. Pay close attention as he states that;

"The spiritual blessings here spoken of are such as are necessary to the perfection and happiness of our spirits; namely, the light of the gospel, the

influences of the Spirit of God, the pardon of sin, adoption into God's family, the sanctification of our nature, and eternal life. **These blessings are here opposed to the earthly blessings which were promised to the natural descendants of Abraham***, the ancient church of God, which consisted in the possession of Canaan, in victory over their enemies, fruitful seasons, as described in Deuteronomy 28. To these, and such like blessings, Abraham's seed, by faith, were entitled by the promise, In thy seed shall all the nations of the earth be blessed. In heavenly places — or rather, In heavenly things, as ɛvτoις ɛπoυρανιoις, it seems, ought to be here translated.*

Certainly, we must enjoy spiritual blessings in heavenly things, before we can enjoy them in heavenly places; namely, blessings which are heavenly in their nature, origin, and tendency, and shall be completed in heaven; **far different from the external privileges of the Jews, and the earthly blessings they expected from the Messiah.** *According as he hath chosen us in him."*
-Joseph Benson.

It is now abundantly clear that all believers are blessed. We are not going to be blessed. We are already blessed. We cannot be more blessed.

We simply need a revelation of what an overwhelmingly wonderful position our Father has placed us in. No wonder why scripture says;

*"But as it is written, Eye hath not seen, nor ear heard, neither have entered into the heart of man, the things which God **hath** prepared for them that love him. But **God hath revealed them unto us by his Spirit**: for the Spirit searcheth all things, yea, the deep things of God. For what man knoweth the things of a man, save the spirit of man which is in him? even so the things of God knoweth no man, but the Spirit of God"* (1 Corinthians 2:9-11, KJV).

Did you catch that? God has revealed them, we are not waiting for future revelation, we should be living the revelation now. Sadly, these verses are mistaken to be speaking of some future event. That is not the case at all. God has unleashed the most powerful truth in theses verses. All that God has for us can only be seen or accessed by revelation from the Holy Spirit. Again, in verse 10 the word says,

*"But **God hath revealed them** unto us **by his Spirit**: for the Spirit searcheth **all** things, yea, the deep things of God."*

May the Spirit of the Lord reveal to your spirit, the immeasurable gift of God inside. May the spiritual blessings be communicated to you now as you read these pages. May your spirit soar to new heights of revelation and spiritual reality.

Notice that the bible uses the plural "blessings" very sparingly. It occurs only 12 times in the King James Version, and just one of those instances appears in this verse, Ephesians 1:3. This Scripture is clearly telling us that New Covenant blessing is spiritual blessing. Not once is the concept reduced to a mere temporal or carnal level in the New Testament writings.

In the New American Standard Version, "blessings" also appears 12 times, and only two times in the New Testament. In this version, one of the verses is Acts 13:34, which quotes an Old Testament Scripture. You can read the entire New Testament, and not once will you find anyone referring to any material thing as a blessing. How amazing! Homes, animals, chariots, money, jobs etc. Not one of these things ever was called a blessing. Not once. This is significant and should not be ignored. Words have meanings for a reason. The early Church had the right attitude and perspective. The real blessing is spiritual. Again, of course, we each need a place to live, clothes to wear, food to eat and jobs to pay for these things, but they are still just things and things come and go. I thank God for all the material things He has bestowed on me. I am grateful for the home to live in and a car to drive but I will never confuse them as blessing. And yes again, the Father knows you need these (Matthew 6:32). So, there's no need to beg and jump up and down in prayer for a job or any of your needs. Just make it known to Him and thank Him while you are about His business.

The only way in which believers differ from unbelievers in this regard is that the Spirit of the Lord dwells within us. We cannot look to external circumstances to discern whether someone is walking in God's blessing or not. Hardship may come and go. Nothing is permanent. No longer do we need to say that God will bless us if we do this or that. No one should keep on praying every time that God should bless them, rather thank the Lord every everyday for the blessings you already possess spiritually. You can now bless the Lord with all your soul. Blessed be the God and Father of our Lord Jesus who has blessed us - by His Spirit. While we thank Him for material provisions, we must never confuse them with the real blessing.

Let us together reject the lie that crept into the New Covenant church that says that God will "bless" us with some material thing or the other if we do one thing or the other. No believer is more blessed than the other. All of us are the blessed ones.

CHAPTER TEN

CHANGE OF LANGUAGE

The early Church was not confused about this matter. Here is part of Paul's letter to a church.

*"For it hath pleased them of Macedonia and Achaia to make a certain contribution for the poor saints which are at Jerusalem. It hath pleased them verily; and their debtors they are. For if the Gentiles have been made partakers of <u>their **spiritual** things</u>, their duty is also to minister unto them in <u>**carnal** things</u>. When therefore I have performed this, and have sealed to them this fruit, I will come by you into Spain. And I am sure that, when I come unto you, I shall come in the fulness of <u>the blessing of the gospel</u> of Christ"* (Romans 15:26-29).

Notice that he acknowledges the contribution for the poor saints in Jerusalem. He makes reference to the financial gift as *"carnal things"* in Verse 27. Not in a derogatory manner but as a matter-of-fact. The contribution was necessary for sustenance but carnal, nonetheless. However, in reference to the church in Spain, he would come to them, he says,

"in the fulness of the blessing of the gospel of Christ" in Verse 29.

It seems clear he understood that they would be blessed by the gospel and not necessarily the "carnal" gifts. The gifts were very necessary. They took a collection and would go to great lengths to deliver the collection to the church. But the gospel was a far superior gift. In fact, the recognizable blessing.

Always keep in mind that even the devil can give money to his friends, but he cannot give them the Spirit of God. He cannot preach the gospel. This blessing is reserved for those who love God, who have asked His son Jesus into their hearts and lives. No counterfeit can match this blessing, and nothing can take His place. Are you a New Covenant Christian? If so, you are richer than the richest person on earth. You are wealthier than any king who has ever walked the earth, except the one who reigns eternally. The church has seen enough people that will give up money so that they will be "blessed", but cannot articulate the gospel to anyone. Such individuals are deficient and bankrupt as far as God is concerned. Their life will not reflect the hidden blessing inside. It is this great gift that we seek the most to convince others about, through our life style. This is better than any carnal gift. No matter how good. No preacher should ever say to anyone that God will bless them if they give. If one does not have His Spirit, it does not matter how much money you give to a church or preacher. You are not blessed.

Anyway, truth be told, not even the wealthiest individual can buy the treasure that we carry on the inside. It is time to walk with our heads held high. We are the blessed ones and we can rejoice in what the Lord has done. And if you are not blessed, this is your chance to change that, by turning toward God in repentance and expectation.

I am coming to you today *"in the fulness of the blessing of the gospel of Christ"* just like the apostle Paul did in Spain.

CHAPTER ELEVEN

JABEZ AND A BLESSED LIFE

Oh, what about Jabez? a friend asked me as I shared this concept with him. I am sure many will have similar questions.

A few years ago, a book came out that promised great blessings to those who would follow Jabez's example. It became an instant bestseller. As far as that author was concerned, if one repeated Jabez's words or prayer, it would change their lives. They would experience frequent miracles and live in God's favor.

The kind of attention this book received allowed any discerning person to gauge the extent of the blessing misunderstanding. Furthermore, it exposed the hunger of the masses of people desiring to be blessed. I am sure the author meant well and truly desires to see the body of Christ blessed. There are valuable insights to take away from the book. However, Jabez's prayer was recited like a mantra and a sure prescription for getting ahead "for God." I do not hear much about that now; although, similar thinking persists, but I will offer these points to those who might ask "what about Jabez?"

Jabez was briefly mentioned in scripture but managed to gain superstardom because of this one writer. What was his accomplishment? He prayed that God should bless him and God answered him. That's it.

His story?

"And Jabez was more honourable than his brethren: and his mother called his name Jabez, saying, Because I bare him with sorrow. And Jabez called on the God of Israel, saying, Oh that thou wouldest bless me indeed, and enlarge my coast, and that thine hand might be with me, and that thou wouldest keep me from evil, that it may not grieve me! And God granted him that which he requested" (1 Chronicles 4:10).

One point made by the writer is this, and I quote;

"Or perhaps you are one of those Christians who thinks that once you're saved, God's blessings sort of drizzle over your life at a predetermined rate, no matter what you do. No extra effort required." Bruce Wilkinson. Prayer of Jabez, page 28.

To which I respectfully say that I am one of those Christians who believes that I am and we are all already blessed according to Ephesians 1:3. Yes, it is that simple with no need for further effort. God has blessed us! He has blessed us *indeed*. He has enlarged our coast to eternal borders by His Spirit. And we do not just have His hand with us, He is with us Himself by His Spirit in us, walking and talking with us. We are making effort to be a blessing and help others come to the blessing! We will not go line by line, but here is just a little reflection over the prayer itself.

"**Extend my boundaries**." As I stated earlier, all spiritual boundries are shattered when we are saved. On the physical level, you might actually lose your life like Steven, Paul, Peter and a host of missionaries all around the world. Many have been burned alive, tortured and beheaded just for the sake of Christ and His Kingdom. But they are still blessed because of the Spirit in them. The work done by God through them continues to speak until today.

"Help me and make me free from misfortune." Misfortunes do not mean that a believer is not blessed. You must know Him in the fellowship of His sufferings and the power of His resurrection. Even in a Setback, trouble or adversity, you are still blessed. I do not mean that it is all about difficulties, but I do mean that even misfortunes do not change the fact that you are blessed. We can laugh at misfortunes. We should not think it strange when we fall into fiery trials now (1 Peter 4:12). Misfortunes may come and may go but the blessing stays forever.

"Without pain" Scripture says *that "it is given unto us not just to believe but to **suffer**"* (Philippians 1:29).

Also consider the scripture that says;

*"when you do well, and **suffer** for it, you take it patiently, this is acceptable to God"* (1 Peter 2:20b, KJV).

Some pain may come your way but that is part of your cross. We enjoy great peace at all times as long as we are focused on the Lord. Pain or no pain.

God has given us good things to enjoy and He protects us from harm. However, we must recognize that we live in a world that does not align with the scripture. Our circumstances at times may be painful, but we are comforted by His Spirit. When Steven was stoned to death, Jesus was there to comfort and receive him personally. Yet he died what we may think was a painful death. Was he not blessed? You decide.

I am not opposed to anyone praying those words, the Jabez words, but with great understanding that we must endure hardness as good soldiers (2 Timothy 2:4). We live in an imperfect world and in fact a world hostile to the word of God. God has blessed us, that is for sure, but we will do well to know what He means by "blessed." We will rejoice always in Him. We cannot be destroyed anymore. Amen. I cannot say this enough. Blessing has nothing to do with material possessions or your station in this life. That is the simple truth. That is the word of God according to the New Testament.

Questions May Arise.

I fully understand that what many have read so far may raise some questions that require answers. I have anticipated and answered some of them in the next pages.

Some may say, what about where the bible says...

"The blessing of the LORD, it maketh rich, and he addeth no sorrow with it" (Proverbs 10:22, KJV).

Yes, you are right, it's in the Old Testament. That would be the context. Riches would be part of the promised blessing and God added no sorrow with it until you transgressed His laws. The nation enjoyed affluence when God's laws were not being transgressed. Personal riches were promised also as a part of blessing. But curses would immediately follow transgressions. Let's consider the following verses;

"...if thou wilt not hearken unto the voice of the LORD thy God, to observe to do all his command-

ments and his statutes which I command thee this day; that all these curses shall come upon thee, and overtake thee: **Cursed shalt thou be in the city, and cursed shalt thou be in the field**" (Deuteronomy 28:15-16, KJV).

Yes, God did not add sorrow to it. The blessing of the old covenant *"maketh rich"*. But curses followed disobedience. Christ specifically has redeemed us from these curses. Again, **we may be chastised by our father when we disobey, we are never cursed**. What a blessing. I think we should stick with the New Covenant. It is better and safer.

One more scripture to consider is in Hebrews 6:7,

"For the earth which drinketh in the rain that cometh oft upon it, and bringeth forth herbs meet for them by whom it is dressed, receiveth blessing from God:"

Here we are being made to understand that, it is blessed to be productive and to be obedient. The earth receives a blessing because it *"bringeth forth herbs"*. The earth is receiving this blessing because it is being duly productive. Blessing here is from **eulogia** {yoo-log-ee'-ah} meaning praise, laudation, fine discourse, polished language, an invocation of blessing, benediction or consecration, a fine speech from God. On the other hand, the land that is not productive after drinking the rain can expect to be cursed. Hence "nigh" as in "near." The curse is the final cutting off of the disobedient and rebellious ones.

*"But that which beareth thorns and briers is rejected, and is **nigh** unto cursing; whose end is to be burned.* (Hebrews 6:8, KJV)

There is danger in receiving the *showers* (spiritual impartation) like the earth, yet staying unproductive. *When we have been enlightened, tasted of the heavenly gift and partaken of the Holy Ghost. Hebrews 6:4,* we must obey and bring forth fruit. We then can expect good pronouncements from God. Like the writer said; *" beloved, we are persuaded better things of you, and things that accompany **salvation**, though we thus speak."* (Hebrews 6:9)

Our Father is blessing us so that we can be conduits of His love and blessing while drawing others to come and receive from Him.

CHAPTER TWELVE

BLESSING IN GIVING

It is more blessed to give than to receive.

The act of giving brings more joy than receiving. Part of your expression of the gift of God in your life is to give. We are expected by God to help the weak. We labor to be in the position to help the ones around us. Not the lazy ones but the less fortunate. The apostle Paul made sure that he showed a good example. I must say that it is indeed an example worth following. We do not have direct record of Jesus making the statement, but Paul lived by it after he heard it,

"You yourselves know that these hands ministered to my own needs and to the men who were with me. In everything **I showed you that by working hard** *in this manner you must help the weak and remember the words of the Lord Jesus, that He*

Himself said, 'It is more blessed to give than to receive'" (Acts 20:34-35, NAS).

The scripture here compares two different acts. The act of giving versus the act of receiving. I trust you will see what is expressed here in these words *"It is more blessed to give than to receive."* It does not endorse or teach that the objects or the gifts themselves necessarily are blessings. Rather, the action of giving is superior to the act of receiving. It can be seen clearly from Paul's argument that he worked with his own hands to be in the position of giving. He did what was necessary to keep things together with his crew. He said,

"I showed you that by working hard in this manner."

He is saying, "follow my example." A true minister that is called by God to minister to his people will be more concerned about giving to the flock than taking from them. He will not leave the weak behind. The weak are not to be abused but rather helped. If you have enough resources that allow you not to work hard, then thank God for it and help the weak. If not, you do the needful. Work. After all, Jesus' words are filled with eternal wisdom. Here, we see that, "Blessed" has the same exact meaning as the blessed in the beatitudes of Mathew chapter 5. Again, makarios in Greek means to be happy. Giving must happen before receiving will occur. *Receiving is great but there will be nothing to receive if there were no giver in the first place.* Therefore, giving is superior and more necessary for the body of believers and for the whole world. There will be no receivers if there were no givers. Receiving ends where there is no giver, right? Think about it. It certainly is a more blessed act than receiving. If most of us would become givers, we can reduce lack. Poverty will be stamped out among believers. As a matter of fact, when believers gave from their heart, the bible recorded that no one lacked;

"<u>Neither was there any among them that lacked</u>, for as many as were possessors of lands or houses sold them, and **brought** *the prices of the things that were sold"* (Acts 4:34 KJV).

Over the years I have heard many preachers teach on "how to give our way out of lack" or "tithe our way out of lack" or "sow our way out of lack." The motive is still profoundly

Selfish. The fact that we receive when we give, does not mean that we are to give solely because we seek to receive. Rather we give because we want to help others. You may not know when you will be the one in need.

"For I do not mean that others should be eased and you burdened, but that as a matter of fairnesss **your abundance at the present time should supply their need, so that their abundance may supply your need***, that there may be fairness. As it is written, "Whoever gathered much had nothing left over, and whoever gathered little had no lack"* (2 Corinthians 8:13-15).

Besides, God in turn looks out for us through others and miraculously rescues us when appropriate. Paul worked to support the weak. Properties were sold to help the needy among the believing community. The act of giving is by itself capable of producing miraculous results. Imagine a church where everyone was eager to give. Such was the case in Acts Chapter 4. Not one time did anyone say that the poor were cursed and poverty was a curse that needed to be broken. They abolished lack and broke the "curse" of poverty by the blessed act of giving. Our giving is powerful. Here's something only a giver can appreciate.

Giving brings more joy into our lives and you will live a happier life when you are giving as cheerfully as possible. Let's give the right way.

The receiver can never be more blessed than the giver. This is a spiritual law. When we give, we look more like Jesus and feel more like Him. Indeed, what a blessing. This is a divinely activated mindset. The Spirit of God motivates us to give by the love of God working in us. We will break barriers and destroy the enemy's chains of limitation when we obey in giving. I am not speaking of giving to buy jets, but I speak of fulfilling needs wherever we can. Helping each other and supporting the weak.

Oh, how I pray that the people of God will live a more selfless life; therefore, making themselves available to be used by our Lord. Give as you have purposed in your heart and watch how God causes others to respond to your needs through the blessed act of giving. It's good to receive but most wonderful to give.

CHAPTER THIRTEEN

CONCLUSION

Please stop saying that God will bless you when you give. You are already and permanently blessed. While it is true that if you sow, you shall reap, one must keep in mind that God has already blessed every saint with His Spirit and deposited every and all spiritual blessings in us by the Holy Spirit. It is out of this blessing that we give and do everything else. It is therefore simply more blessed to give than to receive. We can now bless the Lord and bless people because we are the blessed ones. Therefore, go with God and be a blessing.

Speak the blessing into other people's lives. We may now stop singing Abraham's blessings are mine; instead we now say Abraham's **blessing is** mine. Sure, it makes a difference. Abraham's blessing is the holy Spirit. (Galatians 3:14).

Oftentimes, many think of land and other material inheritances when speaking of Abraham's blessings. But, again and again I will insist that the material part was fulfilled in the Old Covenant but the real blessing touches everyone. The real blessing of God is too much for one person or one generation or one dispensation.

We must appreciate the Holy Spirit as the blessing of our life. We must thank our Father always for his Spirit. Again, I say Abraham's blessing is the Holy Spirit which is received by every and all Christians. We are blessed. I will continue to say it until it sticks with us.

Start all over to fall in love with the Lord and appreciate His Spirit in your life. After all, everyone who is appreciated will ultimately be more valuable to you. Such is the case with the Spirit of God. You must recognize Him as the blessing of your life. As you appreciate Him and spend more time with Him, you will feel more blessed and more fulfilled. He will manifest Himself more. He will overflow in your life touching others around you. He will unleash an unparalleled level of satisfaction and bliss you have never experienced, regardless of what you are going through right now.

Some have neglected to "stir up the gift" that is within them. I will remind you as Paul said to Timothy,

"Wherefore I put thee in remembrance that thou stir up the gift of God, which is in thee…" (2 Timothy 1:6b).

When the Spirit is ignored as we continue to live a life casually punctuated with sin, we run the risk of grieving and at worse, quenching the Spirit. He will become less involved in our affairs. We begin to feel drained, dissatisfied, unhappy and less in touch with God. We are warned not to cause Him to be sad and uneasy with us;

"And do not grieve the Holy Spirit of God, by whom you were sealed unto the day of redemption" (Ephesians 4:30, KJV).

And by all means,

"Do not quench the Spirit" (1Thessalonians 5:19).

When God looks at you on the day of judgment, He wants you to look like Jesus, who is a reflection of His Father. It can only be possible if you come in His Spirit, the Spirit of Christ, the Spirit of holiness. You are already "sealed unto the day of redemption" by Him. Hallelujah! I say again, you are blessed. If you are saved.

The good news is that you are entitled to walk in this blessing because of the New Covenant that we have with God. Stop looking around and being distracted by everything else so that you will be brought face to face with the true blessing of God. How much better would it be to truly know and experience the presence of the living God in our lives? Seek Him with the same tenacity and hunger that we have shown in our pursuit of the ephemeral.

Ask God for His Spirit today, right now and ask in faith and expectancy. You must be filled with the Spirit of God. This is by far the most life changing experience ever known to man. It will also be your most important decision in this life to pursue Him and live with His presence. Is it not true that when we really want something, we keep seeking and asking and knocking until something happens? So then,

"Ask, and it shall be given you; seek, and ye shall find; knock, and it shall be opened unto you: For every one that asketh receiveth; and he that seeketh findeth; and to him that knocketh it shall be opened" (Matthew 7:7-8 and Luke 11:9-10, KJV).

Ask Jesus into your life this moment or renew your devotion to Him if you already are a believer. This is the prayer that is always answered by the Father. Seek Him like never before and you will find Him;

"God is a rewarder of those that diligently seek Him" (Hebrews 11:6).

He rewards us with Himself. That is the highest He can give us for all eternity. It is exactly what He promised Abraham in Genesis 15. He said, *"I will be your reward."* I believe that He is saying the same to us right now. He will be your reward as you seek Him with all your heart. Start living your blessed life now.

You deserve to be blessed, you deserve to have the Spirit of God because you were made in His image. God loves you and wants to bless you if you are not already blessed. It does not matter what you have done in the past or where you have been. None of that matters now. You can be saved and filled with His Spirit. You were made for Him. Your body is His temple. I assure you nothing else can bring complete satisfaction to your soul. Make yourself avail-able now, dear Christian and non-Christian. Submit to His call and give in to His love. Scripture tells us to be ready to be used by Him,

*"I beseech you therefore, brethren, by the mercies of God, that ye **present your bodies** a living sacrifice, holy, **acceptable** unto God, which is your reasonable service"* (Romans 12:1, KJV).

Did you see the word acceptable? He will never reject you if you come to Him in truth and sincerity. This is the acceptable gift to Him. He really does not spend money nor does He eat hamburgers. Your body is His temple and you will only know true blessedness when you bow to Him. God fully intended for humans to feel His presence. You are supposed to feel Him and not just talk about Him. You are missing out on something if you do not feel Him. He is not an abstract God but a forever present one. He wants to touch and bless you with His presence which is His Holy Spirit. His best gift is Himself and your best gift is yourself.

Say the prayer below;

Heavenly father, I repent of my sins and errors. Forgive me now as I come to you accepting your Son Jesus as my Lord and Savior. I believe that you raised Him from the dead as you will raise me too. Bless me now with your Holy Spirit, that I may live a holy lifestyle from now on. A life that is pleasing to you. In Jesus' name I ask. Amen.

INSIGHT PUBLISHING
1600 Flat Shoals Road, SE. Atlanta, Georgia. 30316

Contact the author: upjohn44@gmail.com

www.ingramcontent.com/pod-product-compliance
Lightning Source LLC
LaVergne TN
LVHW051507070426
835507LV00022B/2980